To Betty -
Hope you like it!

Girl...!

SERENITY, COURAGE & WISDOM FOR THE DISSED, PISSED WOMAN...

by Anita Lawson

A. C. Lawson & Collins, Inc.
Chicago
USA

Caution:
**This book uses strong language and
has been rated
"AG"
for
"All Good".**

Copyright 1995 by Anita Lawson
With Contributions by Keesha Powell Copyright 1995
All Rights Reserved.
Published in the United States of America
Anita Lawson
Girl...!: Serenity, Courage & Wisdom for the Dissed, Pissed Woman...
ISBN 0-9647410-3-2
Manufactured in the USA

Dedication

This book is dedicated to my family and friends:
Shelly Boo, Cliffy Poo, Dr. Chuckie, my Dad,
Larry, Keesha, Joe, Alvin, Ben, Nevada, Myron,
Dollar Bill and Momma Lou. Momma Lou is my
constant pillar of strength and support in all that I
do, my personal therapist on call 24-hours a day,
and ...she still makes house calls.
Thank you very much.
I love you all.

Introduction

Poetry has normally been used to capture brief moments of thought or emotion. For this reason, poems have been predominately short. However, being that many of my poems are long, many may say that this book is more a poetic novel, and each piece almost a chapter of a story in itself; I might agree.

With a jazzy new rhythm that challenges the traditional beats and patterns of poetry, poems are again being used to speak for modern problems and circumstances. Just as rap, jazz, country and rhythm and blues recite words that capture the essence of dilemma and heartache, so does this book in speaking for women's pain in the glass house of bad relationships.

With these poems having been called more so performance art, I have placed the words on the page with the same breaks and noted emphasis needed as if it were being performed. In writing this book, I reflected on similarities to Chaucer's "Canterbury Tales" and to Paul Laurence Dunbar's pieces that recall getting up "In The Morning" or the act of wearing a pretentious mask. These two writers both told stories in a poetic format in there own language, that I have attempted to bring forward in my words to the language of the 1990's.

Table of Contents

Page   **Poem**

3   Dear Reader

12   The Itsy Bitsy Liar

13   I Got a Man

18   K-I-S-S-I-N-G

19   I Don't Love Them Hos No Mo'

23   My Little Dog

24   Mr. Bitch

26   Little Miss Muphet

27   News Flash!

28   Take That Shit Back!

31   Little Miss Muphet Continued...

32   He's a One-Woman Man

37   Dear Child

38   Diary of a Gigolo Vampire

42   Bastard

45   Welcome to Hell!

51   Heart to Heart

53   Why?

59   Jack and Jill

60   Recently

65   My Baby

68   Yo-Yo Romeo

76   Your Man...Gigolo Vampire's Baby Boy

84   To My Inspirations

86   Lonely... No! Alone...

87   I Think God's Smiling On Me

89   Thank God For Dad

92   Dreamer

94   Smile

97   Book Order Form &
        Mailing List Application

"God grant me the **S**erenity to accept the things I cannot change, the **C**ourage to change the things I cannot accept, and the **W**isdom to know the difference..."

--The Serenity Prayer

Dear Reader,

To the listener or reader of my poetry
that wish to believe it's all about me,
and with this thought perpetually persist
that ill-fate in relationships simply fail to exist.

To this listener or reader I say,
"I'm simply documenting the history of many plays,
...by men of which there are plenty..."
But, if you wish to blame someone or entity?
Don't blame or look in my direction for me...
God, has granted me with the gift to see,
and document the truth through empathy.

From women who have been both hurt and abused,
bruised of their ego, mind, body and virtue, used.
While many of you may be moved knowing I speak
the truth,
others will cry foul or say, I need time with
Dr. Ruth!

You might smile or declare,
"Another one lost...,"
How simply unfair.
To you, I say, "How brash, your play?!
        You listen contentedly,
        but do not hear what I say.
        Therefore, you simply must not care,
        nor even wish to bare the truth, nor dare.

Girl...!

        Instead you wish to say without heeding,
        that writing and reading
        help me with my lonesome healing."
Yes, accuse me while you're blind,
to what you've tossed and dropped behind,
and of emotions that you're still stealing.
Or refuse to give thought,
that I or we
may have experienced these crassly unjust feelings.

Yes, I may have felt it vicariously through others,
Yes, we are in ways a family of sisters and few
brothers,
with broken emotional ceilings.
No..., believe it's just me!
That is easier to see,
and that this is all about my dealings.
Hell, go ahead it's a free country
read as you proceed
to make me then your little flunky!
But, you fail to even remotely prevail or entertain
that these feelings you have sustained or fathered.
And the slightest remote possibility
that this all happened, leaves you completely
emotionally unbothered.

So, you laugh and try to place me on the defense,
like I'm the rapee and you're the rapist
in a court of which I can't win.
So, you continue to imply that I'm a hater of guys
and men,

or a scorned woman turned lesbian.

While although not,
I harness the strength that they've got
and am a friend or kin to the pain of many and
maybe all women.
Now writing to disrupt,
and make thin comfort levels locked up
of lies used way too often by men.
...in hope that their lies
will run out in supply
and may not be used time and time again.

But the truth about me,
you don't wish to see or accept,
and that is that most men at one time with women
have been inept.

But like Malcolm X
you merely wish to dismiss
me as militant, upset or simply ... just pissed.
Oh, no, don't bother
to look at my poetry for truth;
just do as you had already planned, and will do
and simply deny your selfish way or ill-spent
youth...

Although when Malcolm X lived
a life definitely not passive,
many may not have agreed with what he'd say
in any fashion,

Girl...!

his beliefs or his immense passion...
Then later claimed,
he should have been named
or respected just the same
for having had clear objectives of action.
Or for being educated, a self-taught man
...though through different experiences, and
reactions placed at hand
and having the guts to voice or relay
his opinion found true of his people and his day
in the world.
I now ask you,
"Is this déjà-vous?
and are my views any different in speaking for
females: women and girls?"

But look at you,
after reading my poetry, in view
you're placed on the defensive.
If none of it's true,
I now ask you,
"Why are you now so pensive?"
Looking for an angle to make me mad,
but it's too late, those chances expired and went bad.
You can't hurt me anymore.
My frail body's strong from being sore.
I now see and read you and know what you are,
my soul's now at peace
finally released from the imprisonment of your
webbed lies jar

and having felt the freshness of truth, wisdom and
freedom at their bestest
my soul's now flown far,
beyond were your words could mar or scar.
Yes, but why can't you now confess this.

So, go ahead if you wish
and we'll know as you persist
that somewhere along life's way,
pain is what you've dealt
and you're the one needing help
although you will not say...

Excuse my verse for therapy, healing, ill-feeling or
a sick new method of self-help.

But, I see you move in your seat,
praying I shalln't repeat.
Listening as you then quiver.

"Is the truth too cold?
Or perhaps too bold
Ha-choo!
Ah-ha! I now see you shiver!"

But, stop it's too late
of history to date
of which you may reconsider.
So, you bash me
and my poetry
how remedial, how crass...

Girl...!

Ugh, ugh, not so fast...
Now, I ask,
"Why are you now so bitter?"

Tossing aside women's feelings
gone by,
verbally in your dealings like trash.
As far as I'm concerned,
we've all been burned,
and Hell it's all just one big kick in the ass.
So, go ahead as you verbally thrash
my poetry and feelings you smash without
hesitation or invitation.
Excusing it simply
as is plain for you to see...
...an outdated understanding of relation.
Go ahead as you wish,
though my silence will persist
I see you're verbally trying to crawl up to my
station.

Through my silence, you see, it is plain for me to
see that I am of a higher station!

And look as you go
throwing woman down the road
as they get a day or a half day old,
and with that you toss a new one for old,
as you say, "Another one lost!"
Now, do you see why that statement's so cold?

Yes,
I see you,
as you still too litter.
Then you think to yourself, a therapist or help
I must consider.
Saying to others, "Have you read her stuff?
　　　What did some guy do to her?
　　　Hell, she's all messed up ...
　　　that woman is simply angry and so bitter."

But the truth is, my son,
I might mess up your fun.
One bad apple can spoil the rest of the litter.

But would you care at this point, and try to be fair
for now, the seat in which you sit gets too hot?
But, no I guess not.
What was I thinking?
I forgot.
It was merely a passing stupid thought.
That you may have been born with a kind mind and
gentle... A heart...
...despite how many of ours you've torn apart.

Ouch!
　I felt a thorn!
Was that one there, or did it just form?
Wow,
is it just me, or is the air getting warm?

Girl...!

Yes, my rhyme is like a mirror, of history and of
time,
in which you see yourself.
And each verse, as rehearsed is a polishing in itself
to help remove the dirt by you thrown and by us
hurt felt,
...while you wish to excuse me
as a woman, labeled angry
engulfed in pain and hurt needing healing space or
help.

But to those of you who are inclined to say
that I am merely a woman scorned and turned away
to you I say, "The truth is hard to face.
        It would be for me too,
        if me and my story were in the same
        space placed."

But to those of you
who recognize, I speak the truth,
I applaud each and every one of you.
For you see,
and recognize the truth to be
that relationships may not always be sweet...
Presented as treats, some tasted bittersweet
they then can become hard to eat.

Like roses, we think only of their beauty
but when reaching for them forget the thorns;
we could not see...
for they were not what drew me.

...yet made me sore
but, still wanted
and yes, went back for more.

And to all others
who look at my words and say they're lies and
simply untrue.
I say to you,
      "Peak-a-boo.
      Look at me...
      Boo!
      I think you see, you..."

Girl...!

The Itsy Bitsy Liar

The Itsy Bitsy Liar
did so without guilt or doubt.
Down came the truth and washed the liar out.
Then memory lapsed and memories left in the wind,
so the Itsy Bitsy Liar
did so without guilt again.

I Got a Man

My guy says, "The sky's not blue, it's brown."
My guy says, "Didn't I call you? Oh sorry, I was out
of town."
My guy says, he's faithful to me;
yet, he's known for miles around.

I *know* my baby ain't cheat'n on me.

My guy says, "I called ya, ...didn't you get my note?
Sorry, I stood you up, I was out on a river boat.
Huge as a mansion, it could barely float!"

I *know* my baby ain't *lie'n* to me.

He says, "Sorry I haven't called ya, ... has it been a
month?
Work'in every weekend sure is hard as Hell, hugh?"
My baby works hard everyday of the week,

& I *know* my baby ain't *cheat'n* on me.

Called his house, a woman answered the phone.
Asked him, "Who's she?"

"It's my cousin, friend's wife and she's all alone.
It's only temporary, and she needs a home."

I know my baby ain't *sleep'n around* on me!

13

Girl...!

Called at 7am a mornin',
"Hello..." her sultry voice is a moan'n.
Is he there?
"Yeah," she say,
"He's in the shower, got to get ta work in an hour."

Oh, you lecherous ho!
Am I be'n played?!
Oh, *yeah*...!
Well, not for much mo!
'Cause, I'm out a here!
I got one foot up, and I'm walkin' through that do'!

But *I know* my baby wouldn't *intentionally* be
sleep'n around like a *ho*!
I know my baby wouldn't abuse me so...*you see!*
"Cause *I know,* my baby wouldn't *willingly be...
sleep'n around on me!*

Everyone else could read you like a *book*!
But, it was *my faith* and *trust* that you mistook,
for a fool..., an idiot a *weak fuckin' bimbo*!
For how long did you think you could keep my
whole life in *limbo*?!

You're a lecherous leach, *a fuck'n ho and a cheat*!
My disbelief, allowed you this treacherous feat,
of which I welcomed you into the driver's seat of
my life,
and thanked you to fuck up *not once, but twice*!!

Was my baby cheat'n on me?

Am I just *stupid*!!   Or am I *blind*!!
Can't see forward, only looking behind.
Afraid of the future, yet each time... *welcoming* the past.
But if it was all that (great)...!
Why didn't it last...?

Could my baby have cheated on me?

Got ta move on up and out, 'cause isn't that what life's suppose to be about?
Okay, I'm ready..., ready to move on out.
Oh... and by the way, what's the safest route?

Was my baby lie'n to me?

Okay, okay, I read' ta go.
Oh and by the way what's my guy's numba... do you know?
...not that I'd call'em mind you, it's just for my book.
Maybe it was my actions that he mistook?

Okay, I ready, up and ready let's go!
Sho', gets cold on the open road.
Nice ta have someone you can call...
Do you remember my guy's number, the last three digits or someth'n at all...?
Uh-uh,...never mind!

Girl...!

I see it up there on the bathroom wall...

Maybe my baby wasn't cheat'n on me...

...555-2349, not that I'd call...him mind ya,
just write'n it down while it's still fresh in my mind.
Hmm? Wonder what he's doin'? 'Think it's 'bout
dinner time.
Maybe my baby wasn't lie'n to me.

Have ya got a quarter and a nickel or a dime?
Think I'll call'em just one last time.

Oh... hey, how ya doin'?
I tell you, he sho' is fine!
Stop! What you say? You all alone?
I'll be right there soons I get off dis' phone.
No, I was wrong, ...no, I'm sorry ... I was wrong ...
I'll be there real soon.
Click.
What you say? He's singin' a new song, a whole
different tune?
Naw..., you don't understand him like I do you see.
Let me look in my purse, see if I still got dis key.
Yes! Yip, yip and gota hurry!

Oh yeah..., the road , move'n on and all, will just
have ta wait.
But, our fun little trip down to the path, was first
rate.
And a-a..., notice how I didn't... hesitate.

'Cause, ... I'm all that!
Not take'n it from any man..., none a' y'all!
But, whew! ... that road just seems so long and all...
...and, 'sides...Hell, I got a man at home,...
didn't I tell y'all?
Naw...?

Girl...!

K-I-S-S-I-N-G

Bill and Allie sittin' in a tree,
K-I-S-S-I-N-G.
First comes love,
then comes marriage,
then comes a baby in a baby carriage.

Bill and Jenny sittin' in a car.
Wife's wondering where the Hell you are!
First come lies,
...sex of sorts,
then comes divorce court and child support.

I Don't Love Them Hos No Mo'

Ladies, I ask you, please...?
What is a ho?
A person who fucks for free,
but yet so much mo'?
Without monetary gain?
If you're fuckin' with hos, you're really insane.
'Cause, please believe me although not money,
you're pay'n.
Be that the case, most men are labeled hos
alread(a)y',
Okay!
Naturally fuckin for work and for play.
Stop!
The shit's not okay!
Don't try to rationalize that shit away.
Why...?
They don't need a single reason.
They're a diseased breed, and if you fuck with them
you're sleaze'n.
On foot & bed, they're constantly cheese'n.
They've fucked with my head,
so, now I'm leave'n.
'Cause *I don't love them hos no mo'*

I've decided I'm worth far much mo'.
And now I'm like a kid in a candy sto'.
Deserving of betta'; Hell mo' betta' than befo'.
So, *I don't love them hos no mo.*

Girl...!

Yes, you controlled my mind,
but now it's mine.
Leave'n you, unlike I thought, was right on time,
and now I want a man of a different kind.
So, *I don't get with hos no mo'.*

I thought I'd found someone right for me.
Someone who'd love me emotionally.
I thought you were it...,
but my Mr. Right ...was really Mr. Shit!
So, *I don't get with hos no mo'.*

I have to believe God put me with you for a reason,
to learn that I deserve betta' and ta start pleas'n,
myself.
Yes...,
I'm a funkin' treasure!
A chest full of wealth,
...too bad you were only in it to please yourself,
...without me.
Yeah...to learn the truth, I was pissed,
but kindly hit the door, you've been dismissed...
'Cause, *I don't love them hos no mo'.*

I need someone that's there for me.
Someone who cares for me romantically.
But romance for you was just a funny glance.
Now, I see God's given me a second chance.
So, *I don't play with hos no mo'.*

I Don't Love Them Hos No Mo'

No, now I'm more concerned about what I think or
do.
While all along, you bastard..., you, really knew.
I ignored to accept my intuitions as true.
From the get go, our relationship was already
through.
So, *I don't get with hos no mo'.*

Their price's too high for a fuck in bed.
There price was priceless, they fucked with my
head.
I'd rather be alone than lonely with you, so I'm fed.
I'm through, accepting lies as truth instead,
I've given too much time believe'n that we'd wed
So, *I don't love them hos no mo'.*

It's over. It's over. It's over. *I'm through!!*
Hell, if I had left that decision to you...
You'd still be screw'n me too...
along with the others,
and when I'm gone,
you'll just replace me with another.
So, *I don't get with hos no mo'.*

Hell, now I see it was only a game.
This shit with you was all fucked up and lame.
It's time for me to clean out this place in my mind;
so,... I'm leave'n you behind.

So, *god damn, you;*
god, damn you,

Girl...!

and your little dog too.
Hell, fuck it...
I'm through...

My Little Dog

Oh where... oh where has my little dog gone?
Oh where ...oh where could that man be?

Oh sorry, I slipped.
I don't give a shit.

Please kick him two times for me....

Mr. Bitch

Girl, you know that fool done lost his *god damn mind*!
Goin' behind my back and tell'n those *god damn lies.*
Tell'n people he's done *shit* for me!
That nigga done got me confused with one of his hussies.
Walkin' 'round dishin' out all that *shit.*
I tell you I'm through and I'm not *hav'n* it!

That nigga done lost his *god damn mind*!
He's left me behind so many times...
...the strength of my mind is all of how *I've* survived!
And yet, he's still talkin' shit and tell'n those *god damn lies*!

Talkin' 'bout *bitch* betta have my money, ...you hear what I'm sayin...
Mr. Bitch think *fuckin'* with me is funny?
Workin' hard for him, he thinks that shit's for *free*!
The work I do ain't for free; Hell, Mr. Bitch betta have somethin' for *me*!
You hear what I'm say'n, hun?
Mr. Bitch betta go and ask someone.

Mr. Bitch thinks he can talk like that to me?

24

Mr. Bitch

Hell, he must think he's in the wrong *fuckin'*
country!

He ain't given me a *god damn thang*!
Then he come talkin' 'bout how he gonna give me a
rang.
Then I really thought about it, ...you know what I'm
sayin'?
Hell, I don't really want that shit, 'cause he's still
playin'.

Talkin' 'bout how he's gonna give me 4 out a 7
days.
And then with the others he's gonna split the rest of
his lays.
Shit, I thought God must have put betta for me
under this sun!
And, Hell...,
I'm tell'in you, shit...,
Mr. Bitch... betta go and ask someone...

Girl...!

Little Miss Muphet

Little Miss Muphet sat on her big rump
eating her foolish pride.
Then came Horny Horner
that sat down beside her
as he began and continued to lie.
One day she stood up and realized he was fucked
up,
and told him to kiss her ass good-bye.

News Flash!

Little Horny Horner sat in a corner,
'cause Miss Muphet wouldn't come out to play.
When contacting Horny Horner earlier for
comment,
he replied, "I have nothing else left to say..."

Girl...!

Take That Shit Back!

OPP is the *Fucking National Anthem* of men.
You think by now they'd try to ascend up the ladder
and try to do right.
But no, and I tell you ...that shit sho' is tight.
You heard the story of the Black man's plight?
Hell..., if you ask me, they're askin' fo' that fight...
Ain't nothin' but a mirrored version of what he's
doin' to the Black women or wife.
Married or not, he'll fuck up your life.
Oh ,well...
It's not up to me;
I think why there's a Hell, it's plain to see,
But, I ain't got no reason to lie.
I'm not a salesman with a product to sell;
no, to me that wouldn't apply.
(I'm) just a person with experience and a whole lot
of truth to tell.
The Black man needs to recognize he's taken the
test and failed,
and so stand tall and take that shit back!

Oh, "No?"
Well, not to worry, God's taken care of that.
He knows most men are nothin' but crap!
Throwin' lies, on top of lies; trash, no problem, will
compact.
Not ta worry, the shit is coming back.

Take That Shit Back!

Oh, "No?"
Here we go...
over and over again.
Correct it now, or you'll only continue to descend.
And you'll always be talkin' 'bout what you
should've *had*... and could've *been,*
until you take that shit back and do it again!

'Cause until you do right by me, you'll never win!
Until you do right by me, the ice you're walkin' on
is thin!
Until you do right by me, don't talk to me...
You have no case to plead; I mean that
emphatically!
But don't dish it out to me.
'Cause I no longer eat *crap*!
So, you just take that shit!
You take that shit back!

You think God's blind, and he ain't got no eyes?
You think God's a guy, so for *you,* ...fairness don't
apply?
You think God's deaf, and he ain't got no ears?
So you can lie to women in
...God's house,
...your bed
and sleep with no fears of lies that you've said!?

Well, you're full of shit!
Take that shit back!
'Cause I'm done with it,

Girl...!

and I'll have no more of that!

You cry about the Black man's pain....,
but it ain't nothin' more than your lies
comin' back in a *boomerang*!
'Cause if that's all you are to *me*?
I'm better off with a gigolo,
they require a *lesser* fee!
And you'll always have the Black man's pain,
Until you end this reign of lies,
...and *shit* like that.
'Till then, you'll always have pain
and pain is *fat*!
You *wezafied* little *fucked up* rat!
Until you take that *shit back*!

Little Miss Muphet Continued...

Little Miss Muphet couldn't wait to pick up
and embark on a new and clear day.
When then came a liar that sat down beside her
and convinced her to live life his way.
So she gave up meat and her precious Opera seats
for the promise of a life with him.
Then when she wasn't looking,
she found he was booking
other women to cater to his whims...

the end

Girl...!

He's a One-Woman Man

He's a one-woman man, from Milan to Japan...
that means he has at least one woman in every city
at hand;
he has realized the old-fashioned way,
that it's hard to lie and remember what you say.
So, if there is only one in each city,
this adds to life just the right amount of spice,
for us what a pity...
And really one is all you need to suffice
at least for one night, I know most guys would
agree that I'm right.
Then he can take each one out
and to the city he then will proclaim and shout
that he has found happiness and knows what true
love is all about
and that his heart is no longer starved.
You're love has given him a brand new start, and
that you're his soul's food, his edible.
And tell you you're his world and so damn
incredible.
But, he can say these things all day.
No other's feelings will get in the way.
...another perk of the job.
Traveling to London, Paris, Brussels and Bombay.
For without the threat of each one meeting the
other,
there are no feelings to consider...

He's a One-Woman Man

Ahh...doing it in the same city could make feelings
bitter,
and would be such a tremendous bother.
Wow!
Wouldn't he make a wonderful father?!
Although on his shoulders these matters have no
bearing.
Isn't he so nonsuperficial and caring?
So, he can make it seem as though he respects your
virtue.
And he can lyingly vow to never hurt or desert you,
and make you believe those old love lines, like
"You're the only woman in the world," are true.
Little do you know he's got two more loves in Peru.

He's a one-woman man, from Canada to the US.
It's unfortunate for us, he says he likes the US best.
Oh yes, for us the constant pressure and the stress,
having peace only if he'd confess.
And yes, if he chose to acquiesce
But, we know better girls,
if he comes clean here,
he still has 20 more in the third world, my dear.
so, we choose to play this game.
Even though we recognize that nothing's changed;
and knowing what's up as you see him off from
plane to plane...
nothing's gotten better, it all remains the same.
The only place it's changed is in your mind.
Closing doors to reality so that your eyes may not
see,

Girl...!

nor allow yourself to realize
what you know the truth to be.
Proclaiming to yourself, it just isn't so,
and lying to yourself that he is your best friend, not
your worst nightmare, enemy or foe.
And for all intents and purposes, you've gone
emotionally blind.
Convincing yourself that his old life is behind.
But did he ever make any commitment to change?
Hell, he sees it all as a rather exciting game...
Life is good for him;
Look...you've remained!
No...no rain has hit his party or parade.
So, he of course has chosen to continue this charade
and whenever possible to increase his escapades.
And you have chosen to become nothing more than
a pawn on his chess board,
with power to move but one or two steps forward.
Recognize that you have done this to yourself,
and that within yourself is the true help.
You've given all your power away,
while all the other pieces on the board control and
set the game.
Pull back and instead chose to be the queen!
...who moves freely every which way and will
control the board or make a scene.
And when pieces get in her way she simply moves
them off or tosses them away!
Notice how she can do this with every piece
including the king, without his wish or say.

Ever recognize how the king on the board
may only move one space toward any one direction
per play?
This is because of the bones and skeletons in his
way
which impede his progress every step of the way.
But for the queen it's not this way nor is it true.
In fact, the king with his limited power attempts to
stay close to you
to protect him from the other queen from across the
board: i.e. the other country.
Notice how games begin to mimic fact, life and
reality
and as unexplainable as placing your life on the line
via jumping, bunjee.
While never once considering to elicit the rights of
a treaty.
He loves the game, the hunt, he's too carnivorous
and it's all deliciously meaty.
So, while you pretend to be a pawn, the truth and
secret is that you're a queen,
protecting your king so he may continue to do these
obscene things.
But you need to let him go and use your power for
you
and leave him to the other queen's wrath or torture
for abusing your virtue.
You need to recognize what is true and that you're
in command.
Even though he claims with you he's walked the
burning sands,

Girl...!

the truth is the only way he made it was by holding
your hand.
To this I know you must now understand and relate.
So walk away and hear in the distance a voice cry
"Check-mate!"
And know that this fate was impending
and so deserving with him having been so
condescending.
So, look away and do not lie to yourself or walk
through life pretending
that your relationship simply needed a little
mending.
Because the truth is your relationship never offered
an array for beginning
but was instead in a state of perpetual endings.

Dear Child

by Keesha Powell

What are you searching for, my dear child?
You are tearing yourself apart...

You won't find it in your make-believe world...
You see, there lies your worst fear....isolation.

You won't find it in another man's love...
You see, there lies your worst fear...separation.

You won't find it in another man's kindness...
You see, there lies your worst fear... betrayal.

You won't find it in another man's bed...
You see, there lies your worst fear...emptiness.

You must wake-up, my dear child!
I'm begging you desperately.

You must wake-up *now,* my dear child
or you will never see... the true *happiness*
...that is you.

Girl...!

Diary of a Gigolo Vampire

Yes, I am a man with females that I have sired.
You all know what I am, and yet no less desire,
to quench my thirst,
and yes, to breathe my fire.
What I wants not your love, just lust required.
Give me your life, your blood and we'll then
discuss.
Give me your trust, your heart... now that is a must.
Say to me, "Take my virtue, if you think you can."
That's when I know I've got you right there in my
hand.
You know there's not just you,... I'm the man in
demand.
If it is me you want, you must walk the sands.
If you live to tell? I might kiss your hand.
Come to me now and know that you'll never reign.
If you do, do this now... then you are insane.
That is when I'll know I've got both your heart and
brain,
then I shall place them both in my locks and chains.
Into my darkest kingdom you will then be placed
along with the others you fight for me, now... this
you face.
Learning your trip with haste was now just a waste.
Maybe next time you'll learn to have better taste,
but this lesson although learned, it is now too late,
and you still run to me and for all else hesitate.

Diary of a Gigolo Vampire

That's when I know I've got your trust and sealed
your fate
Maybe next time your mind will pick a better mate.

Ah, now it's time you approach the flames still grow
higher.
As you move into my world, "Do you feel the fire?"
Look as the flames grow bright and they then will
swirl and whirl,
that's when you know you're in my darkest world.

Ah, and yes... dark justice has now been fairly
served.
For it is danger's game requested and once reserved;
therefore your screams,... cannot now be heard,
but for this you asked and now your answer's sired.
Then know it was a *gigolo vampire* that you're heart
has hired.

Watch as the heat from lust has now got you wired.
Yes, he is straight from *Hell;* so, now feel his fire.
Other guys young and old see his women and
envision,
that they can too be like him, is a firm decision.
It is him they envy; this to see is plain.
The fact that women did make and still make him is
truly insane.
All of the little boys want to grow up to be just like
him;
thus we have the cycle repeat time and time again.

Girl...!

Although you know pain and lust are what he now craves,
be his and you can too clench an early grave.

Give him your heart then wonder why you are now cold.
He is a *gigolo vampire* and you were surely told.

If you wish to release the spell before your virtue's sold,
take your heart back and stab him with truth's dagger and end this show,
but only if you think your heart and soul do both matter more.
Then serve him his lies, back on a silver platter.
If they're not lies, don't fear he shalln't get any fatter.
Then walk away and leave him there to feast in peace,
for he's not mortal, he's a ravage ghastly beast!
Then as you walk on out of his chamber door,
turn around and see him squirm with his lies once more
But you now look upon him with truth's clearer eyes
seeing the true monster you wished for... but don't be surprised.
You just regain your confidence and say to yourself once more,
I deserve better and set your eyes on that front door.
Then do not watch, nor feel, as sorrow's tears do hit the floor.

You should now rejoice, because you're soul's
released, although bruised and sore
as you now walk out of his now crumbling castle's
door.
Because you now leave with your soul in tact and at
peace...
The game is over, your soul's regained... heart and
mind are released
and you shall pray to God, thankful you've reached
the shore
and pray there you'll stay forever and ever more...

Bastard

in the aftermath of betrayal by affair
i looked in your eyes to recognize
that no one was there
then i pulled back to see your stone cold face
as i covered mine and cried with bitter disgust and
disgrace
and recognized for the first time i saw no soul in
you,
no, no one was there, no there was no trace
and i cried
because you lied
(and you said i simply needed to try a little harder)
and i thought i was special to you
but now i see how easily i could be replaced
and i continued to cry because the truth was hard to
face
and instead i saw you'd lied so well as you do, do
placing me under your spell with your South
American voodoo
and all along to find that my intuitions were true;
my hands then pulled from my face
as i thought, "...how could you?"
and although hesitant, in haste
i said, *"...god damn you!*
...you lifeless bastard!"
and wished the truth's pace would slow, but no, it
still came faster,

and for the first time i saw how you covered your
path,
looking at the truth in the blind shine of this
aftermath
moving on to the next one, you told her i was crazy
and that in your next conquest you had found your
true lady
and you will play her too
like you did play me
of this i know it is definite
there is no maybe,
to reflect i remember you said you wanted my baby!
now i see it was just to have sex without protection
how wise of me to have voted differently in this
election,
when you had the second baby, i knew something
was wrong,
that thought i should have pursued, but, no
everything appeared where it belonged,
when you named the first one Déjà,
i should have recognized that the second one's name
was Vous
but instead i thought, "no," and still wished not to
see the truth
but how sad i am for the other two women with
babies you have fathered
i see now it was simply a matter of a condom with
which you didn't want to bother
what a large commitment to make for sex
if i had known that then i would have been upset

Girl...!

but now that i have had time with my bitterness to
reflect
i see now that you are a master of lies & decept
and with these other women i
now understand and sympathize
because i once was blind
but now i have finally realized
that you are a *bastard*
a wolf in sheep's clothing
of which your lies are constantly unfolding
and you are a bastard that is now plain to see
and now i know the truth,
it was you... not me.

Welcome to Hell!

Welcome to your
bus ride to Hell!
Enjoy your ride,
all hands inside,
and please provide another kiss and tell.
Careful, watch your step,
yep, yep, yep.
Haven't you found a good man at church yet?
Hugh?

Welcome to Hell!
Take a seat,
though bittersweet, still what a treat,
oh, don't look so surprised,
...and well, well, well...
29 of our passengers shared the same guy!

Now, there , there, there,
please, don't cry,
just dry your eyes and realize
that all the signs of betrayal were there.
Where, where, where,
you then say?
Just look down the path, there are crumbs all the
way.

Ahh...
and has this guy called you yet?

Girl...!

Don't worry you've got your seat here
and now you're set.

Collecting your tickets to Hell!
Thank you, hun;
I'll take that one.
Oh look right here,
your ticket was prepaid!
...way back in August on here it states.
What you remember in September was your first
date?!
Now, wait, wait, wait...
but I'm so sure you'll just toss this one up to an ill-
faded fate.
He knew you were coming here on day one.
Admit it; he's a bastard, he's a fuckin bum!

Well, well, well...
It's sad to say,
before he had
either met to relate he bought your ticket on that
there date.
He had already made and paid for your reservation,
thus, avoiding both commitment and
confrontation...
But, thus giving you a whole lot of aggravation!

But, you'll love your time in Hell.
Better than a jail cell,
you'll love the heat,

and some will repeat.
You know our service is number 1...
the best thing under our sun, and still it can't be
beat.
If you need something, just yell or ring my little bus
bell,
then advance and kindly take your seat.
Just how long will you stay? Did you say?
We haven't got there yet
and you must go a long, long way.
Wouldn't you like to stay several weeks and a
holiday?
Now, just wait and see,
while I begin to peruse my sheet and see where
you'll be.
While some of you will stay a year or more...
other's will be here a day or just a week.
Oh, so short, oh what a bore...
Parting is so sad, but bittersweet.
Oh, look! ...on my sheet on this line,
...says this girl's guy cheated on her nine times!
But, what she doesn't know is that in Hell she's a
star!
Messing with this guy that claims he's a bachel(a)r.
'Cause although he claimed he was single, even that
did vary
(he was married)
and you know this bum got married not once, but *12
times in Gary*!

Stand up for this one, hun!

Girl...!

You know who you are.
You know you're the one.
Well, in Hell you're a Superstar!
And let's all give her a round of applause...
Yes, she's been through the male version of JAWS
and for that you have won a little prize,
to help you to continue to socialize, hun.
Oh, see isn't Hell just lots of fun!
Here you are
now you're ready for your next fucked up bum,
...oh... I meant guy.
...got 'a love 'um, they just lie... and lie.... and lie...

Please do, unwrap your gift, although it's no
surprise,
but maybe you should sit, before you open it
You know what it is...; it's ... *a personalized shit
and toilet kit!*
So you can constantly take his shit then dispose of it
and the pile shalln't get any higher.
We think it's a wonderful gift,
compliments of us, your friends on the bus,
and of course, it's manufacturer, Hearts on Fire...
I know your so happy,
you think, "Oh, no this can't be!
This guy I loved was taking pure advantage of
me?!"
But, yes he did and here it is on video, just for you.
We watched it right here in Hell all on channel 22.
And look and see right here it says or does it say,
that today is in fact your *anniversary*!

Welcome to Hell!

What elation!
Oh, joyous day,
how rare it is, a double occasion for celebration!
And of this I'm sure we will see your next episode
on Hell's hot and steamy TV station...

We're now approaching the doorway to Hell.
Now enjoy the tour,
be pissed or sour,
but keep your feet both on the floor.
Careful girls as we go through the anger cloud of
steam.
Sit still, please, this gas will pass just like a dream.
When you exit our bus please don't forget our
frequent traveler application.
Because, I know many of you will be back, to join
us for another vacation.
So, for your convenience, please call and book your
next reservation.
Please do this when your guy gives you the slightest
implication.

Now, look to your left to see our biggest attraction.
It's the machine that made the guys that put you all
in traction.
Oh, don't you just love our guys?
They're great... they just lie... and lie... and lie...
It's our male asshole machine,
which you all do claim you love our new models
and fashions

Girl...!

I'd not be surprised,
if all your guys came from this machine,
and are sold from this very wholesale store or so it
seems.
Tell me girls how much was the price?
...at retail... or would you pay much more or twice?
...were the models both smooth and yet work
precise?
Ah yes... you say they worked quite enticingly nice.

Now we approach the gate to Hell,
and is that your heart and mind that I think I smell?
...burning for him still?
Do you know you're in Hell; do you want another
stupid pill?
You're at Hell's gate, wake-up, and be for real...
Yet, you still feel it's not too late, he was so
wonderful ...a fuck'n steal!
And you and he can make up and then off you two
will go.
You still blame yourself, for what I do not know?
But, don't let me stop you,
or tomorrow there will be no show.

You're still playing yourself, no matter... there, there
and off you go.
I'm not worried; she'll be back real soon of that I
know...

Heart to Heart

Words can pass through lips
causing ego trips,
while claiming to sip
and have savored life.
But when the lips yield to the heart,
a new conversation starts...

As you begin
the heart awakes
to rehear old words
once said, but not really heard
now said again, to both fight and defend
and all other hearts then snap to atten-tion.

You can tell a guy good-bye
look him straight in the eye
and tell him to die
and go straight back to Hell.
But be it truth or lie
it's a serious apprehension, bound to fail
if they're just words...
For without the heart, you cannot make the sale..
The pitch!
...you know the one right after he returns the favor
and tells you to pickup your clothes and please go,
'cause it's safer
than talk
or cheaper than a trinket that he just bought.

Girl...!

...by avoiding heart to heart conversation...
Do you know and understand my rationalization
or what I mean when I say...
that without the heart to speak for you,
you have just talk without passion.

Why?

Like a snake slithering in and out of lies,
or just as sand through an hour glass...
So are the days of our lives, apprised of so many
malicious lies.

I ask for the truth and await with no reply,
and continue to watch as the lies *pass me by* as
easily as a grain of sand
passing through an hour glass or through the *fingers
on a hand.*

All the time in my mind, *"Why...?"*
...asking *"...why?"*

Finding no comforting answer on which to rely,
No, no, ...not of which my mind can supply...
and still hesitating to ask him,
"...well, should I?"
And even if I did, I would not get rid of the
questions that pound in my head,
remembering the little things that he said,
things that at the time seemed to have come straight
out of the blue,
now seem as though they are the only truth I ever
knew.
Although he did not admit them as truths at the
time...

Girl...!

Funny how lies can be clarified with time, once
allowing the truth to unwind.

Looking at myself for answers on any angle.
Thinking, "Was I not pretty or smart enough?" in
these hypocrisies I got tangled.
Tough?
I think to myself, ...waiting for myself to *shut up*!
And still I find myself asking, *"why?"* ...although
I've had enough...
It's these questions that can beat ya down,
long after he's left and is no longer around,
an attempt at reconcocting yourself, as if by a brand
new chef,
no, no, ...nothing of which like the one he's left.

As though he's the supreme being of what is
worth... or worthy of love, honor and respect.
But I'm so pissed and puzzled...
Hell! Don't get me any more upset!
Looking at this mess, just praying for some bit of
self-worth!
Yet each time like a vine weighted to my waste,
each thought of his-story pulls me down in haste.
Reflecting on how he treated me like dirt
and in the end him knowing that I'd be hurt,
...and still he didn't care.
...I know ... no one said life was gonna be fair.

But like a rose bud that has not yet sprung into
bloom

in the garden or in a spare room...
only to rise...
and surprise...
every onlooker from sunup to sunrise...
This bud's for you! *...ya self-conceded bastard...*

How I could not have seen the demon that you are?
How I could have allowed our relationship to go as
far as it did... *ya selfish pig.*

You never gave a thought about I, me or we,
or what might proceed your malicious self-centered
actions.
Yet even to this day you still lie to my face, not
even giving me the dignity or grace
that I thought a person of my long-standing in your
life would deserve.

But still you did, I tell ya cuz ... I guess you weren't
the person I thought you was,
who wouldn't do but most certainly did and does...
Word!
Now finding new truth in all the whispering that I
had *heard...*
Hell, the fact that I would even think that thought
that you would not...
...well, that shit's simply for the birds!
No! You are *not* the person I thought you was or
were,
Truth comin' so fast; Hell, the whole thing's a blur.

Girl...!

Trying to believe that only something so rare and so special could have enticed you now seems absurd, and yet the simple unfortunate truth would have sufficed
your hard blow to reality quite nice-ly.

And still I haunt myself with these questions of "why?"
> Why did you leave me?
> Why did you deceive me?
> Why didn't you believe in me?
> Why wasn't I good enough?
> Why wasn't I made of finer stuff?
> Why couldn't you have told me the truth?
> Why couldn't you have just let me go
> > and then pursued
> > someone
> > or someones...else?

But, *no!*
You wanted ta *just use me like a ho'!*
Thinkin', *"What the fuck! That's what girls are made fo'...!!"*
And this mentality seemed to fit so nicely into your plan.
Making me think I'm the one at fault and then you're the one in command.
But I wanted to believe it was me, because that was sadly enough easier to see.
And I wanted to believe I was wrong, because blame in my life had there always belonged.
But you continued to lie again and again...

Why?

Whatever worked best by whim and then
shortly after, throwing caution to the wind.
And with each lie when caught to his face, then
came a little laughter.
That's when he knows he's been caught, I then wish
you the best of luck.
Another lie will soon spurt up and out, right after.
So, if you want to survive you best just duck!
or else catch another lie, ...*of which they are not in
short supply...,*
right in the eye.
But that was my problem, letting the then thoughts,
now lies go on by.

But when finally seeing the many lies for what they
were as they lie before my face,
each thought although haunting becomes less so,
and some how easier to place.
As I finally experiment to learn that *shit don't fly*!
And for each good thought, I find 5 new bad ones
once covered by lies,
now unraveled by the truth to remove their dirt and
disguise.
And relearn that I to me, am, have and shall always
be, my strongest source of strength.

And the once teary eyes lying awake asking,
"why..."
now awake to find new power in the truth that you
rewrote to soothe yourself ta boot.

Girl...!

And my "why's" asked to no reply now take on a
new attitude of
"Hell? Why ask why?!"

And the once sugar coated memories of you
become newly bathed in salt and now taste sour
even to the sweetest sweet tooth.

And my previously undaunted belief and trust in
you,
become replaced with a new unpinkened view.
The jolt from the truth knocked off my rose colored
glasses of you
of which they cannot be replaced upon my face
because the impact from the fall threw
you *crashing* from grace and broke those glasses
smashing lens and all to the floor...

And you will never, ever look the same to me as
you did...
...befo'.

Jack and Jill

Jack and Jill went up the hill to have a little fun.
Jack forgot his date with Mill
Now he's...
outnumbered 2 to 1.

Girl...!

Recently

it recently occurred to me...
that maybe i should shut my mouth indefinitely
and silence myself to walk through life quietly

is this not the plea of many men
who see my words and then choose to defend
their own words to the bitter end,
then pray for my silence adamantly

and then...
it recently occurred to me...
what if i listened to what men wish to say
and allowed their words to wash all my doubts
away
would everything then be okay?
would they choose not to walk away,
only to play with another female filet?

then,
it recently occurred to me...
what if i am wrong
and put most men in a category where they don't
belong
what if all men are really good and not evil
if it were true, would it or could it even then be
believable?

what if i am making stories up like in a book

and it is my imagination that requires a second look,
is this not what you men would want me to believe
is this not the way you continue for us women to
deceive?
it's almost like placing or concocting a spell
and sending us all indirectly or straight to Hell

then...
it recently occurred to me,
that this is the way men like to play this game
and if i were to believe this shit, i would allow them
to put me to shame
even though it is them that have been cheating on
me, playing me like i am to blame

see if this sounds a bit familiar to you:
"Damn it Sue! I've been sleeping with her... but I
made love to you.."
"Yes, I may have been with her, but now that stuff
with her is all through!"
"Hell, I don't even see her that way,"
which number would she make then in your play
book of plays
when you say,
"You know that I love only you in that special
way."
see this is what i call believing what you want to
believe
if you had any sense, you would pack your things
and right then leave in your defense

Girl...!

because deep down you know you've just been
played for a fool
and the sad reality is that you have just been raw-ly
schooled
and you know it's true
Hell, you're dealing with a pro, girl, of that ya
should now know,
you need to walk away and let that shit go

how you gonna think you can trust that sad excuse
for a man
Hell, he's still runnin' around from bed to bed with
his pants hangin' down,
you want to believe you got something special, but
you'll be paying life's tab
but while your back is turned he will continue to
stab...
you stay around long enough all you'll get is a bad
case of the crabs
and then he'll come talkin 'bout how he got that at
the gym
then you're the fool, if you again choose to believe
him

it recently occurred to me,
that what if i'm right
and men do lie for each other,
in order to avoid our fights
what if in the male mind, we women have no rights
and this is the only justification they need not to
limit their sights

on every cute little skirt that passes him by
and hence we have their justification to lie

it recently occurred to me,
what if being quiet and walking through life mad
is how men keep us all separated and treat us bad
and thus no one talks to the other
this allows them to play the same game and pass to
each other's son or brother
and through generations these games go,
the same tired, mixed-up lame games
okay...ya know
which none of us wish to recognize, because of their
low blows
i don't believe i've ever heard one of those hos
apologize
and for what?
they really don't have too
because for every woman that leaves, a new one
comes, of this they have realized
believe'n that she's got something special,
"Hell it's that foolish pride!"
God forbid she loves him, then he'll send her heart
straight to Hell
and then we've got the other group of women who
believe they can change a bad man to good, ...with
sex
don't you know he's not changin' unless he elects?
how you think you gonna change him with
something he's already got?

Girl...!

you think you're the only woman whose gonna put
out for him or that's hot?
you betta get with the program and realize... *not!*
and that with this plan you haven't got a shot

it recently occurred to me...
that men are masters at deception playing us against
each other and ourselves
even though we know the truth, it's hard to admit to
ourselves that we've failed
and finally admit that there is something wrong with
the male version of the man
and instead of kicking the other woman who didn't
know about you or his male
revue or show
calmly speak to her and then the truth you both will
know
and then maybe we can finally end these one-man
shows
'cause what he's got ain't all that hot or special either
you see
i think it's time that the truth set us free.

yeah,
i think my first thought...
you know, ... the one before the stupid thought
where i gave men a shot ...
was right ...originally.

My Baby

When I first met you,
you seemed a dream come true,
patient and seemingly shy in virtue.
I could see in your eyes
that you'd never lie... I thought,
nor would he willingly hurt you.
So gentle you seemed, could never be mean
and in this I thought you were weak.
But what a surprise
when I'd opened my eyes
to learn that my baby was freak!

From bed to bed,
...although nothing was said...
I guess, of this I should have known
when he'd left me alone
and then reeked of a different cologne,
not realizing it was perfume and cheap.
But I sure should have thought,
as he spoke of much needed stock
and purchased 4 big cases of condoms.
But how could I know,
he was just giving a show,
of this I denied or at least had assumed,
...you know...
and the truth I did not wish to seek for fear that it
would be too bleak.

Girl...!

But I guess I sort of thought, "why?"
when he looked in my eyes
and said these cases were just different balloons for
Trick or Treat.

But I should have cried foul
felt in the deepest of bowels
when we got in bed and he gave me head.
Yes, I sure should have fled
when it was plain to see, that of this act he'd
improved drastically.

But then after a sigh
reaching orgasm time after time
my lips then tried to cry, sh-h-h "...foul play..."
but then my mind thought, "...no, ...why ask why
and spoil the show?
Why not just save it for another day."

As I thought and did shed thinking, "m-m-m...
words better not said..."
and wrote off the matter, as his new found
mystique.
As I turned over in a stupor in bed
I thought, "okay,
...tomorrow will be the day I will call him a cheat."

But then I thought to myself, "...well, think about
this before you do.
Is it my conscious or his I want to soothe?"
And then thought "Hell, ...I know the truth!"

And tomorrow came and went.
And each day was ill-spent
on a nonexistent relationship spawned by
uninhibited youth.
Just sex! ...in every place and room!
Hell, we even did it outside in a telephone booth
and on the roof!
"Oh, dear... I fear ...did I just share too much?"
...okay...
...well... of that, I'll just shut up and hush
I guess there is ...no need to rush..."

But I felt like a fool, when placed in the front row
of life's school
where life surprisingly was worse...
You know...
where everything happens without being rehearsed
...where the lesson comes second and the test is
first...
and then thought, "Oh well, don't bother, you'll
surely find another...
...you won't have that long to search," and then
thought to myself, "...what's wrong now?
...he's just a jerk!"
As I reflected, "Yeah, but...
that's six down and counting...
...from *church*..."

Girl...!

Yo-Yo Romeo

Yo-Yo Romeo, who was that girl I saw you with at
the picture sho'?
Yeah! Lookin' pretty chummy, you know you
were.
When you whispered in her ear, ...*what'd you say to
her*?

Yo-Yo Romeo, what would Juliet say if she were to
know what I knew?
Tell me, Romeo, is it true?
...that you pledged your undying love as clean and
new?
And that she's the only one in your world for thee?
...interesting, how one's world, once small, grew
large so quickly.
Are these facts?! ... Dear Romeo?
Come on... pretend for me, just like you did for her.

Yo-Yo Romeo, who were you with at the play...
Hugh?
Oh, no...
Juliet didn't go...
Oh, *come on*, please tell.
Oh wait! Another kiss and tell!
No,
let me guess,
hmm...well?
Was it *Jezebel*!

Yo-Yo Romeo

I think she's hot.
What! You say, with her you were not!

Oh stop, Yo-Yo Romeo.
You can tell me,
and no one else need know,
nor will they require a plea to defend.
...although we both know you're as guilty as sin.
What, did you say, I'm creating lies again.
No, its not that way, it's you instead
claiming your love is never-ending.
See! It is you who are pretending!
...to be a friend and befriending...
Poor-Poor Juliet,
so sweet, so kind, so tending,
that you tend to forget,
yet, that's not what you see.
Instead you see a sure bet,
and a woman so depending,
her problems can go without mending,
and so they do everyday.
You must think she's such easy prey,
and...she's the most trusting of kin, so you sin,
and still claim together you ride,
...while your *dick* blows off in the wind on the side.

Yo-Yo Romeo!
Don't stop! You must be having so much fun.
While thought
to have only one.
What truths

Girl...!

for many you have shunned.

Yet if Juliet only knew what I know...
Do you think she'd stay, or would she go?
Would she realize that a prize, she had not won,
"What?
You say she was pregnant with your son?
And herself she would kill
to keep your good name from shame, she must be
ill...
Oh yes, I meant what devotion.
Her love must be deeper than an ocean...
to protect you from (any) implication,
Could you do the same?
Hugh?
...too bad you do not share the same relation..."

Yo-Yo Romeo!
Wait a minute..
I've seen that play, it's featured again...
where Juliet killed herself at the end.
Now I know it was your dignity she was to defend.
Wait...!
You're still here!
Correct me if I'm wrong, but weren't you to have
killed yourself (too) and shared a song?
No, need to correct me, another lie or untruth.
Don't worry I understand now, it's just you.
Another lie coated with a slight truth,
...especially liked by girls in their youth.
Those pills, you know, go down so smooth.

Yep?
Your pill box must be running on empty,
with women wanting not 1 or 2 but 20.
Oh, yes, wanting plenty to pretend they don't see
your behavior...
Quick!
Another lie to savor!

(just like Shakespeare lied without waver)

Yo-Yo Romeo!
I just want to know do you ever favor,
...with women, do you have a favorite or dislike any
particular flavor?
Ahh, you say, "Yes."
But let me guess, Juliet didn't understand you, nor
was she the best...

Yo-Yo Romeo!
Is it the hunt?... the game?... that you're drawn to.
Oh, with many loves for different seasons,
so many acts by you, each year committed of
treason
...of the heart; I ask, you, "... still what's the
reason?"

Oh, Yo Romeo, you're so smooth you would not
tell,
and you can go straight to ...well.

Girl...!

Still you say its not true.
Well, who was that new girl I saw next to you
at the opening dance,
as you lie about her or did she stand a chance
of a broken heart and a plastic love sick romance?
Tell me, did you get in her pants?
She's oh so pretty.
Let me guess?
Hmm?
Are there still others through our fair city?

Yo-Yo Romeo!
You are dangerous and that is plain for me to see.
Yes, you've learned that romance is the key,
and yes, ahh... slightly witty.
Hmm...
what a waste, what a pity...

Yo-Yo Romeo!
How did that line you recited go "You are the only
woman alive for me, my love runs so deep and
enduringly. Please know my love for you is pure
and true and in my world there is only you."
Yet it still remains to be seen or true...
who in heaven allows you to do the things you do?!

Yo-Yo Romeo.
Moving up and down like the host of a game show
in progress.
You have too many women in excess.
You're a walking devil...

Yo-Yo Romeo

You're a demon in white dress.

Yo-Yo Romeo.
What!
You say today's the day you will retire?!
Oh, interesting, for how long?
...might that be for an entire hour?
...not even 8, just long enough to regain your power
for your next hot date?

Yo-Yo Romeo.
Does this mean you will any less desire...
or cancel your date with Samson's Delilah?
Oh dear, Yo-Yo Romeo,
watch your step
for I fear
the close of your show is drawing near.
Wait, I see you step into the fire.
Wops! Did I push you?
Oh, watch!
What a ball!
Look! You burn like alcohol!
Watch the flames go higher and higher!
I think I'm feeling slightly queasy, excited or tired.
Oh...
It was a dream.
I guess it's just a way to release a little steam.

Yo-Yo Romeo!
Your days are numbered, and when they're up,
I see you in my mind all fucked up.

Girl...!

Oh, what fun, what a rush!
Oh and by the way, have you seen the movie, *Fatal Attraction*?
I think you will evoke the same type of reaction...

Yo-Yo Romeo!
You're looking for the seed in the seedless cherry bowl.
Although you don't know,
in every bowl of cherries, there is bound to be a hole,
...a single seed.
But one of these is all you'll really need.
So, don't stop now.
Maintain your lack of control!
Pick another woman,
you're on a roll!

Yo-Yo Romeo, how many more women do you think you can merely disgrace,
while all along you place a smile on your face?
You've started the countdown and increased the pace.
The countdown has begun.
So, Romeo, watch out for number one,
'cause when she arrives,
she will explode like a loaded gun.

Yo-Yo Romeo.
There they go, count them, dearest Romeo...
5-4-3-2

Yo-Yo Romeo

hun',
haven't you guessed yet?
I'm number one.

Girl...!

Your Man.........Gigolo Vampire's Baby Boy

You women like to talk as though you're strong,
but you're still *weak*.
Oh..., so tell me...
Am I *wrong*?
"Yes?"
Words are so cheap...
Otherwise, into your consciousness and bed I could
not creep.
Leave me like a poison in your mind and there I'll
seep.
Then willingly give me your heart, because you're
so selfless, in your mind
well, for a while...
I'll take a bite and toss it left to my heart pile,
that's why some call me no less than A heartless...
but, don't you start, you're in denial.

You know I'm carnal, I quench your thirst, and
when I'm worse
You like it more, each time for you is just like a
first.
Don't talk, don't move, stay on the floor.
You're nothing more to me than a whore...

Tell me... what do you think I use you for?

...been with you 2 days, need another, because now
I'm so bored,

too late to react, you said you knew the score by far
before.

So, I walk into a bar
and there...
yes, you all are.
Oh, such willing prey,
...for me you are.
Waiting to accept my play.
"Bartender, please bring the lady another shot of
Tangeray!"

Hungry, you are, for me just like a Snickers or a
chocolate-coated candy bar.
I don't even need to approach you, ...although I do
do that too.
But there you are...
In my trance,
...shall we dance?
Kindly take my hand and still you advance.
Your eyes look into mine, a glass of wine & things
are fine.
Half way through,
I know, *I've got you...*
body, mind and soul, so cheaply, I bought you.
and so, I took, with just a look.
Thank you for your contribution to my black book.

You like it...
You love it...
Oh, yes... you do!

Girl...!

But easy does it or you'll be a shell,
...no...
Oh, well...
Why don't you leave me and tell me to go back to
Hell?
...and then we're through...
Is that what you want
and want for me to do?
No. I didn't think so.
'Cause you cannot leave me, you know its true,
you can't,
or should I say more so that you sha(ll)n't...
'cause then I'll still be in your mind and I can screw
you there well too from behind.

Who will be next in line?

Contemplating to stay or go, this happens to me all
the time...
Love me, or leave me...although I can't tell you
what to do.
"A bit of advice... most do pursue..."
Although you'll say I mus(a)tn't,
you'd like to think it's just me, pure evil or voodoo;
Oh..., I see.
But face it, it's not just me, it's you...
who allow me to do the cold things that screw you...

See, you come to me,
still hungry and you thirst;
just as I do for you...

Your Man...... Gigolo Vampire's Baby Boy

...well, at least at first.
But even though I lust for you, I don't care.
Although no love in my heart is there.
You say, "Yes..." but I ask you...
"Where? ...humorously where...?"

Some how, you'll convenience yourself, again, that
our relationship is fine and fair...
and share your blood,
your life, your essence,
although this parting is hard for you to bare!

But since I have none,
I want more than some & I don't care.
I'll pierce your heart and instead of some,
...well, you'll trust me...won't you, hun?
And I'll let it come & go, flowing 'til your life
blood's all gone.
And tell you that you're the only one...
but adultery is already done.

Blood and treachery are so much fun...

I'll clear your body of every single drop.
And that's when you will yell, *"No! No! Stop!"*
...but, it's too late and in reply I then say,
"So..."
Oh, you give such a brilliant performance in your
show.
"What is it that you don't want the world to know?"

Girl...!

Once so self-assured, and giving and all that stuff,
after me all that shit will go,
Yes, you're all fucked up, heart empty, mind fried...
Now I've left you all cold and dry inside.

Look...!
Now, you're just like me you're the walking dead...
So, now you too walk in the darkness of the night
and jump from bed to bed looking for the light
or Mr. Right or at least you think you do.
What you really look for is Mr. Right Now... to
soothe you.
Not marriage, just sex, not to wed...God forbade.
Now you grab the meek, the weak to be bled and
then you too will be fed.

Yes, you walk in the darkness, without a tear left to
shed.
You prey on the meek and are now among the
walking dead.

Look, the moon is full and it is now time
to take another victim; I'll attack her willing mind.
Come out at night,...they do
stalking me for action,
and there you are again mistaking me for passion.
I'll be just what you want me to be,
no matter how well you love, you see...
when I leave I'll still be empty and free...
still empty inside lonely for a new heart.

Your Man...... Gigolo Vampire's Baby Boy

Will it be yours... this time that I'll tear apart?

When there's a full moon,
I'm at my best, you try to test me and you'll play the fool.
You try to trap me with a baby as a willing tool.
How stupid...and for the baby, how cruel.
You think you can rule me with responsibility?
Then you're stupid and what you should have done was flee.
You think I'd stay 'cause you're havin' my baby?
Then, lady, I think it's clear that you're the one that's crazy.

You say you do not want me,
yet, for me you still thirst;
and I feel my ability to quench your desires first.

I want a heart.
I'm cold inside.
Come in my plane; so, I can take you for a ride!
Hands off controls!
We're on a roll...
But, stop! I've got seats empty were not yet full.

Now, we're off!
Wait! Don't close that door!
I need just one more thirsty whore.

Although you won't admit it ...
What do you think I use you for?

81

Girl...!

Forget Mr. Nice and pay my high price.
You can be with me, if one night will suffice.

You still want a slice of me?
Well, pull up to my table, ladies,
and make a bid to pay my fee
and if you're not there, "...good ridden, ...who
cares."
"oh, how unfair!" you say.
Then you won't too share today...
the grand prize, which, of course, you see is me,
nor will you enjoy another one of my notorious
fables,
but I don't care.
You see... I am the son of greatness, *Cain,* not
Able...

Every man looks at me
and wishes he too could be
and have all the women I have...
...thank you, ladies.

'Cause without you,
I'd have no one to screw.
And if one leaves, then here come two
...more willing victims
and she'll swear that her love is special and rare.
I don't remember saying life with me was fair and
then I'll taunt,

tell her she's right and then she'll give me what I
want.
I'll steal her heart,
and throw it with the rest.
Yet, still each new one will swear I won't and then
attest
that she knows what's best for me and still lift up
her dress, you see.

But that's what I want!
Don't be so surprised.
'Cause if you looked you'd see it right there in my
eyes.
So you can't cry, when I say to you "...good-bye."
And you learn that my every word and words were
nothing but lies
and make you wonder.... "why, oh, why...?"
and think on your mind you just can't rely, but you
still will aspire
and will no less desire
the next cunningly attractive *gigolo vampire*!

Girl...!

To My Inspirations

You might think my dedication
goes out totally to my book's inspirations.

Well, although one's name is spelled
M-I-C-H-A-E-L,
you may also know him, although differently his
name is spelled.

Might it be B-R-I-A-N?
Oh, yes.
...but don't think I'm coming back *again*.

Or might it be C-H-R-I-S;
well, don't believe I'll be back to complete your *test*.

Or might it be J-O-H-N?
Well, I'm tired of hearing lies and then trying to
defend them.

Or might it be T-E-D?
Well, believe it; "You've seen the last of me!"

Or might it be L-A-R-R-Y?
Well, I'm tired of crying lying awake asking why?

Or might it be R-O-N-N-Y?
Well, I believe we've said our last good-byes.

Or might it be S-A-M?
Well, I'm tired of catering to your ever whim.

Or might it be E-R-I-C?
Well, believe it baby, you've knocked some sense
into me!

And yes, if I may be so bold,
despite how they're *spelled* ...they're all pronounced
COLD ASSHOLE.

Girl...!

Lonely... No! Alone...

I'd rather have no one, than have someone who
doesn't care.
I'd rather be alone, than wait for someone who's not
there.
I'd rather talk to myself than talk to a voice without
an ear,
than awake one morning to find absent love has
disappeared.

I'd rather have no love than a love that doesn't exist,
than to play with a superficial, nonexistent,
consequential pretense.
I'd rather hope for a love that's true to me,
than awake each morning to an ill-faded dream of
which I persist.

I'd rather awake to a field of possibility,
than to sleep in a world of ill-willed reality.

I'd rather be alone, than at home waiting by a phone.
I'd rather be alone, than lonely at home...

I Think God's Smiling On Me

When the times are bad
and it seems that life is tough
and you are about to yell to the world that you have
had enough
and the path which you go down seems both rocky
and rough,
then look to the sky and see
the rain has stopped from pouring and
a rainbow has appeared and now seems so alluring.
That's when you know something seems different
and therefore reassuring
when you can look to the sky to see the clouds so
clearly.
That's when I think God's smiling on me.

When life seems painful and everything but cheery
and your young or old bones seem so tired and
weary.
That's when I look to the sky and think,
"...that God what a wonderfully great guy," and
breathe in the clear blue sky's air,
even though I may still think, "Life how simply
unfair."
I know that if but for a moment or always,
when the sky is blue and the air is clear
and the birds about me sing with laughter and cheer
and the warm bright sun has again blessed me with
his grace

Girl...!

as I feel his warmth shine down upon my face.

I think right then, it is plain to see,
that I think God is smiling on me.

Thank God For Dad

My heart goes out to my Dad.
The best Dad a girl has ever known or ever had.
He built up my belief in myself,
and then like a book I placed it on the shelf.

My heart goes out to my Dad.
A selfless man, the last one; oh well, I guess that's
too bad...
and now I'm reflecting on back when,
I had something worthy,
a best friend.
And still repeat..., make a wish and pray, there one
will be.
Still when I open my eyes,
no one is there, and I'm still empty.
Oh yeah, right!
Then I'm suppose to believe that they care?
Psyche!
I'm so shocked, what a surprise, *the truth's a fucker
to bare.*

Selflessly loving, my Dad.
Can't find a man that could repeat that,
and oh, that's so sad.

You want me to have faith in men?

But, when will their faith in me begin?

Girl...!

Selflessly, wonderful... my Dad.
The only way he'd leave me is that he'd die, he's dead,
Oh, yes he did, and that's so sad.
But try to find a man that will repeat that dedication...,
Your answer is SPACE EXPLORATION!!

Wonderful Dad.
A girl can dream all her dreams and awake to think that men have class.
Where did all the good men go?
I fear that by women,
they've all been leased, lashed and trashed.

...and wonderful Dad.
Gave nice guys a name that could reign and yet still pass;
where did all the good men go?
Do you know?
Or is it that we walk by them like a misty gas...
looking for someone else who's mean, selfish and crass...

Wonderful Dad.
I'm sure he'd say find a good guy, ...now off you go.
But go where, please tell me, do you know?
And then that's where I'll be, that's where I'd go.
And then we would see,
if anyone really has the key to unlock my heart.

Or will another fucked up relationship stem or start,
Or is it just to me that all this seems...,
most guys are nothing but talk, not thought or act,
just steam.
Oh, well...
Hell...
I can still dream.

Dreamer

by Keesha Powell

I lost myself in a picture at the art museum.
It was a couple.
They looked very nice.
It was a sexual kind of picture.
As I looked at the picture, I labeled each color in
depth with the feeling it displayed:

>Black is the war of their inner emotions
>White is the coldness in their hearts
>Yellow is the excitement in their minds
>Gray is the sadness throughout their bodies
>Red is the pain experienced through
>courage
>Blue is the serenity that will follow the
>storm

and just think all these colors are beautiful to me...

I better get home before I lose myself again.
It's gray outside and I have to ride the bus today.

As I was riding home, I lost myself again.
This time in an Essence magazine, in another
picture.
This picture was simple,
a beautiful Black man, woman and child ...all
wearing birthday suits.
The colors in this picture were just as simple as the
picture itself:

92

Dreamer

Black for the beauty
Brown for the security
and White was the bond they shared

I better be going now before I miss my stop.
You see, I'm a dreamer... and I just might lose
myself again.

Girl...!

Smile

It's a morbid kind of happiness that makes me smile
then hesitate for a flashback of an old lifestyle
...left some time ago,
seems like yesterday, but isn't so.

It's a morbid kind of laugh that makes me smile
of a time which was good to me for a while,
but then I had to see,
that what seemed right, could not truly be.

It's a morbid kind of joy
that makes me remember,
the good, the bad, the not-so-bad, the sad...

But these memories were given to me
and mine to keep for all eternity...

...it's not over,
'til it's over...

Book Order Form
&
Mailing List Application

Instructions:

<u>Mailing List</u>: To be placed on the mailing list, please complete the following information & return it to the address below.

<u>Book Orders</u>: For book orders, please calculate the total due based on the information provided & send the total due with your mailing address to the below listed address.

Name: _____

Address:_____

City:_____ **State:** _____

Zip Code: _____

Phone Number: (   ) _____ - _____

Sales Tax:
Please add 8.75% for books shipped within Illinois.

Book(s):
Number of books _____ multiplied by $13.95 per book.

Shipping:
For fourth-class shipping, add $2.00 for shipping
the first book and .75 cents for each additional
book. Allow 2-3 weeks for delivery.

For priority shipping, add an additional $1.50
per book. Allow 5 business days for delivery.

Payment:
Make payment payable to:
A.C. Lawson & Collins, Inc.

( ) Check   ( ) Money Order   ( ) Cashier's Check

Mail To:
A.C. Lawson & Collins, Inc.
575 West Madison Street, Suite 351
Chicago, IL 60661